ANOTHER 100 QUATRAINS

(Yet Another Rubaiyat)

Richard Chandler

ISBN: 9798685072436

Layout by Rachel Greene for elfinpen designs.

Cover by Amelia Greene.

INTRODUCTION

Like so many poets I've always been fascinated with the Fitzgerald renditions of Omar Khayyam's *Rubaiyat.* As a young man I was taken by its Epicurean bent and Ecclesiastical themes, and there are certainly echoes of these in these modern quatrains-- in fact, so imprinted is Fitzgerald's impression, that sounding no echo might prove deleterious. The one 'shadow' quatrain in this collection would surely be counted so (I love writing about shadows, being one myself).

In later life, I was somewhat unnerved to learn that thousands of Persian quatrains have come down to us, that Khayyam's are forever in dispute, and that even the ancients argued over literal and symbolic imagery (when in doubt, it's both). The key to the quatrain is of course its immediate impression—if not a lightning flash, then ball lightning, maybe. Its assertive design precludes the interrogatory; you accept it or you don't, like speed dating.

This collection was written in August, 2020, during the shelter-in-place dictated by the pandemic, which no doubt set the tone for several of its verses. The unusual rapidity of composition mirrored that of its predecessor, and this might suggest how Rumi would compose over a thousand—as with iambic pentameter, the poet adopts the technique with repetition, in a sense learning to see his topics in a quatrain-tinted lens, more or less.

In this case the challenge was less tonal than topical, and the choice of subjects often dictated the angle of approach; and as it is with haiku the question is of suggestiveness—if a poem isn't resonant, it hasn't fully disembarked. These verses hope to lead one to another, like seashells on the beach, and that with the tide of times always coming in.

As with my previous rubaiyat I have included brief commentaries to accompany certain verses—in part because, what wouldn't we give to have comments from Hafiz or Omar Khayyam? The brevity of quatrains precludes self-elucidation, and while it's part of the charm, it's also frustrating. T.S. Eliot was a lifelong admirer of Khayyam, and said the poet still eluded him even in old age--and since Eliot continues to elude me, maybe a little more clarity all around might do well.

THE QUATRAINS

Dreams leave indistinct the borderline

Through which the past and present intertwine;

Some pose a riddle, or end in the middle,

Or posit a question by symbol and sign--

Dreams that go forward,

                        and dreams that lead back

To times when only the Devil wore black--

Do they prognosticate about our fate,

That's coming roaring towards us down the track?

It's early in the journey—we embark

From our apartments while the sky's still dark;

The moon has not yet set as we go on,

And those awake have still not heard the lark.

Look to the past to understand today,

The lessons there will navigate the way;

Look to the future, for nothing is new,

And nothing you find around you will stay.

We gather round for an unguided tour,
But just where we're going, nobody's sure;
The maps they sell here show someplace else--
We can't tell where we are, nor where we were.

If possible, live your life without regret;
If not, then learn to forgive and forget--
Yes, this advice has been around forever,
And still, so very few have learned it yet.

You fall in love with eyes above the veil,

Alluring as the temptress in the tale--

Those flashing eyes have always been distracting,

And any defenses erected still fail.

It may not be responsible, nor wise

To stare into the beauty of those eyes--

Yet if they're just a glimpse of paradise,

Then giving in is hardly a surprise.

We look into the past, and we pretend
Those halcyon days never had to end--
And with contradictory evidence
That better days are just around the bend.

This may seem overly pessimistic, and perhaps this is colored by the 2020 pandemic and its social and economic impact—but the general sense of this quatrain is always with us, and it's common to see the past as rosier than it might have been. There's an endless appeal to nostalgia, especially at so distressful a time.

From womb to tomb, it may *seem* doom and gloom—

But that cannot be all, we must assume;

There must be more before we're out the door,

Before we're swept up by the passing broom.

Remember always, faith comes first and last

When you're negotiating with the past--

A little candle flame is all you need

When the moon's new, and the sky's overcast.

You slowly step along the narrow lip

Of the thin edge, knowing that if you slip

It's one unending, perpetual fall--

All things considered, hardly worth the trip.

These days it takes more discipline than Zen

To calm yourself, when troubles come again--

The days will never be what they had been;

They'll never be the way they were back then.

Another day begins, with or without you--
Some will support you,

                others come to doubt you;
Another day starts the usual way--
You don't know what's coming,

                but you're about to.

This very early quatrain speaks to a familiar foreboding brought on by the recurring challenges of 2020—one of the hardest years globally in living memory. The sense of fatigue in the verse mirrors the apprehension that abides through every day of this awful year.

The morning concerns assemble and gather,
The busy gossips dissemble and blather;
Every day we do what we're told to do,
Too few of us free to do as we'd rather.

The hurly-burly of the morning rush,
Arriving early to the morning crush,
And so soon you're thinking Tahiti thoughts--
Or anywhere quiet, leafy and lush.

The summer morning roses in their bloom

Afford us more than beauty and perfume--

They offer glimpses of a grand design

That ardent astronomers only assume.

But every day we see the planet turning

There are more ships sinking, more towers burning;

Lessons around us surround and confound us,

And still we so very little learning.

Whatever you so carefully conceal

Is nothing valuable enough to steal--

Everything's trash, and it's gone in a flash,

And nothing in this haberdashery's real.

Whatever you so skillfully revealed,

Adds up to nothing when your time's repealed--

However well you came to play the game,

Another team steps up to take the field.

We strive to be just and hope to be wise--

It's only over time we realize

That even at our best, we only guessed;

How well we did, we can only surmise.

There's nothing predetermined in our lives

Except, perhaps, when the sunlight arrives--

Our future's ours to fashion as we may,

And whether someone takes a dive, or thrives.

It doesn't take a psychic to foresee

That we cannot predict what is to be--

The past is hard enough to understand;

The present, like a lock box with no key.

It's like we're living in a little box

Closed up and secured with multiple locks--

There's a thin slit up top, like a child's bank,

But there's no door, in case somebody knocks.

No-one explained to me where the time went,
Or how recklessly my time had been spent--
We're on this level plain for just so long
Before we begin that long, slow descent.

This was the first of these quatrains to be written, and from it several quickly followed, suggesting that this form wasn't done with me yet. It also occurred virtually word-for-word, which happens very seldom for me, and I find unsettling when it does.

In our beliefs, can we ever be certain

Until the Showman opens up the curtain?

The swami seems to levitate at will--

Isn't he weighed down by our common burden?

This may not work, I know—the idea is a little nebulous, I admit; but I just wanted the rhyme, and something had to pay for it! I had wanted to rhyme the word 'turban', and that just made matters worse...well, now nobody's happy.

We're justified in having our suspicions

About the dicey side of our conditions--

The game we play's already underway,

The books we're in aren't subject to revisions.

"Yesterday's always better than today"--

Or so naysayers and pessimists say;

Only these days, can you deny that phrase,

Then times are bad, and worse is on the way?

We're separated for a little while
During this dreadful global term of trial,
And now, even being close enough to touch
Seems almost as far as a country mile.

This is clearly referential of the 2020 pandemic. We are a gregarious species, social and communal by nature, and it goes much against the grain to stay isolationist for long—the months of sheltering-in-place put upon us by the virus has been hard on everyone. (The 'little while' referred to in the poem was wishful thinking, sad to say...)

If you and I should ever reconcile

After such harsh words, and such a long while--

Should we own up to mistakes on both sides,

And ever meet again—why then, we'll smile.

I've made mistakes and faced the consequences

That came with admitting to those offenses;

I've made the fine for stepping out of line,

But now they're out of my daily expenses.

We need our hope to compensate and cope
When we're about at the end of our rope;
But how do we climb up through such a time,
When hard rains batter this declining slope?

This is another instance of a verse simply unfolding all at once, like a Japanese fan; I jotted it down once I could, and needed to change only four words, which is remarkable. Why this happens, I'll most likely never know, but I'm appreciative.

How does someone live a good life today?

Should you give all your possessions away?

And if you took a guess and got it wrong,

Will there be some serious hell to pay?

If hiding in the past has cost you nothing,

And loaded dice you cast has cost you nothing,

Then is there any risk? In fact, there's many,

When the path chosen last leads into nothing.

I miss the breezy freedom I once knew
When I'd brush by these summer roses with you--
But while this isolation lingers on,
Such memories as these will have to do.

I've searched from Indonesia to Iran,
I've searched from Argentina to Japan--
Looked all around, and I still haven't found
A single clue to the eternal plan.

If there's a reason for the stars that spin

In this little universe we live in,

We might comprehend why we start, and end--

Why such a curious dance might begin.

Perhaps creation is inherently good in-and-of itself; still, even if it is, why is our universe designed as it is? Why is Time one-way? If we knew there was a Heaven, wouldn't that inspire us to resist evil (the knowledge itself wouldn't preclude free will)--and while we're about it, of what use is evil, anyway? Yes, there's faith—but again, why must there be?

Do you believe love's in the scent of spring?
Do you believe love's cause enough to sing?
For if you do, I hope I'm just like you,
And still believe love's all and everything.

Don't question very long how you should live,
Open your heart, offer your hands, and give;
You cannot keep these days—they're granules
That dissipate one by one through a sieve.

We've lived in this division for too long,
We've tolerated too much that's gone wrong;
It's time we overrode this cynicism--
Let others own up, step up and be strong.

Is there a reason why evil exists,
That's long since lost in primordial mists?
Is there some purpose obtuse and obscure
That still eludes us? The question persists.

We're sinking in a vessel made of lead,

And soon there's only water overhead--

The course we charted was flawed from the start,

And now we're headed for the ocean bed.

We feel alone in this terrible time,

As if we'd committed some terrible crime--

And once on the hook, the judge threw the book,

And these prison walls are too high to climb.

We can see better days, but they're still distant;
We'll reach them finally, if we're persistent--
We've taken the first, most necessary step
In recognizing what is precious, and what isn't.

This summer could be glorious and green,
The loveliest my days have ever seen--
And yet, while you remain so far away,
Nothing this summer will leave me serene.

On a round table covered with green felt,
You're in the game to play the cards you're dealt,
But never planed to drop hand after hand--
You should have hid one more card in your belt.

I never intended to let you fall--
I never intended to bet it all
On numbers and colors not on the wheel,
When you were the pit boss, making the call.

I've stolen moments, and I've stolen kisses--

My passions have been mostly hits and misses;

Each day I navigate past love and hate,

And slip the narrows of their interstices.

At midnight, when half the restless city slumbers,

You're at the safe, listening for the tumblers;

Life's always like this—everything depends

On hitting the proper sequence of numbers.

The pirate ships are hidden in the cove,

Buccaneers searching for a treasure-trove--

The only gold here rides along the beams

The gild the palm fronds in this open grove.

In Haiti, voodoo rituals and rites

Still echo restless through the moonlit nights;

Dances and chants, pins in effigies,

And fabulous and forbidden delights.

The solar system circles til its done,

Its planets all subsumed into the sun--

So, did this dance just come about by chance,

Or was there some reason this wheel was spun?

Why is this endless universe so vast,

Its galaxies spinning away so fast?

Why set in motion this eternal dance,

Started in an inconceivable past?

Parallel universes intersect--
They merge and diverge and interconnect,
They say, who believe they crisscross and weave;
But there's no proof—not even indirect.

*Well, not yet...! If creation if indeed
infinite, then sure-- multiverses, scads of
dimensions, sub-atomic physics, and all
that... It's already unnerving to consider
how incredibly small we are, and infinite
anything is unimaginable; so, why;
moreover, does 'why' even apply?*

There are enigmas we will never solve,
No matter how far our kind my evolve--
The mysteries of time, and faith, and meaning
Will baffle us until all things dissolve.

A raindrop on the surface of the ocean
That goes unnoticed in the current's motion--
This world is a raindrop, the sages say,
Is an after-thought of a fleeting notion.

The fortune-teller making her predictions

Knows the majority of them are fictions;

They just pretend to know

what's round the bend--

Even foresight comes with some restrictions.

If you transform by the light of the moon,

And not yourself til the next afternoon,

While on the market, silver's on the rise,

Don't feel alone—none of us are immune.

Deep in the woodlands a humanoid shape,
Too large for a man, all wrong for an ape--
The jury's out without more evidence
Than some dark figure on videotape.

*Perhaps I should apologize for this—only,
I'm not sure to whom...I don't believe in
Sasquatch personally, mostly for
anthropological and historical reasons; but
many people do; and if I'm proven wrong, I
hope it's from a considerable distance.*

The wisdom we all commonly inherit
Will always be scrutinized for its merit--
It's all too easy to simply accept,
Or just repeat it back like a parrot.

I've finally written down all I know
About the afterlife, and where we go
When we're done here, then above, or below--
Blank pages scatter where the four winds blow.

Ancient Egyptians offered up to Isis
Their freshest harvests, and their rarest spices
For just a little comfort in their lives--
What did they offer, when facing a crisis?

So, who hasn't always wanted to dedicate a poem to Isis? She remains the longest-lived—that is, worshiped—deity from ancient Egypt, unless there's some obscure cult favoring Anubis somewhere...and some see her as inspiring early Christianity (which I doubt the goddess herself would approve).

A new-made poem is a will-o-wisp

On twilight's edges, when the air is crisp;

Sometimes they're eloquent once they arrive--

And sometimes they stumble, and sometimes lisp.

These verses may be written from the heart,

But poets would say, that's only the start;

Infuse imagination with a purpose,

Compassion with beauty—that's art, in part.

Poets are children in a candy store;

Just offer something good, and they want more--

The walls are language, the shelves full of rhymes,

And images of spring adorn the door.

I promised one day these verses would stop,

And someday I will just let the matter drop--

Poems are like those luminous balloons

That shimmer in the sunlight, til they pop.

The image in my mirror isn't me,
I don't see how it could possibly be--
I'm someone who has hope for the future,
Who's nothing like this impostor I see.

My shadow wants nothing to do with me--
It wants the car, and the apartment key;
And now, it's issued a formal decree
That I should let it go, and set it free.

I wonder if these verses are worthwhile,
Or have they gone forever out-of-style?
I wonder whether they're a waste of time,
Like arrows missing targets by a mile.

Are you and I added to the same list?
Is everyone on it—was someone missed?
We should be updated, once we insist
To see the record of who may exist.

We either turn to faith, or turn to science,
Who still comprise an uneasy alliance--
Sometimes you lean on one, sometimes the other,
And sometimes both will require compliance.

We argue and defend unsound positions
We're often supporting unstable decisions--
We're off in a brew of our own delusions,
Like crossing the Arctic without provisions.

It seems as though I've written this before,

As though exploring a familiar shore--

Well, if it's true, and I find nothing new,

I won't be traipsing that way any more.

The wisdom of the ages—maybe not;

The wisdom of the sage is polyglot,

And as I progress, I learn less and less--

The wisdom in these pages? Not a lot.

Do you believe angels watch over you,

That divine intervention's overdue?

Will we embrace their celestial grace,

And might there be angels we never knew?

Those who don't know mostly chatter and chatter,

And those sycophantic flatter and flatter--

But those who deny it mostly stay quiet,

The ones who address the questions that matter.

Does what we do down here mean anything?

Each summer and autumn, winter and spring

All that existed recedes into mist,

And not a clue what tomorrow will bring.

This is adapted from lines in two odes by Hafiz, in a similar way that Edward Fitzgerald created many of his quatrains. It's nothing new, sorry to say—and while I can't read Persian, I'm certain the lines read far better in the original.

It may come quickly, sudden and abrupt--
A lightning-strike, a stroke, a poisoned cup;
It seems we come to chase oblivion,
And no accounting, when your number's up.

*This verse was written around its third line,
which kept recurring til I built it a home--
then it settled in, and I could put it behind
me. The Keatsian phrase of 'reading by
lightning' comes as close as any I know to
what's done here, hence the lightning
image.*

I fake identities as if a spy,

My forged passports and papers, all a lie--

I've always wanted to be someone else,

Always disguised, and hoping to sneak by.

You welcome unexpected summer rains,

Yet the high heat of summer still remains--

Don't tell the baker to set aside shelves

When you haven't yet harvested the grains.

The following quatrain is another expression of those regrets that never seem to rest. It's human nature to second-guess ourselves, especially in later years; but it's harder still, when you repeat past missteps, and you should know better—sometimes, you do know better...

I'm watching my options circle the drain,
And since it's my doing, I can't complain--
Still, there should be exceptions to the rule
That once we're through,

        we can't go through again.

The fallen leaves are scattered red and gold
In the first winds of the autumnal cold,
The season's beauty spins up its full height
Before the claws of winter's taken hold--

Under the green lines of the autumn mosses,
Looking out over the white lines of crosses,
This terrible year leads us like the Piper
he way we come to consecrate our losses.

These are written for the 2020 pandemic, in memorial of those many thousands lost to us.

Khayyam instructs that only ruby wine
Will inspire communion with the divine--
This may have worked for him, but I don't find
A link from drink to any grand design.

Hafiz had written how roses and wine
nfuses every individual line
        With the immortal breath of the divine--
I know I'll never claim the same for mine.

In the midst of the carnival commotion,

A charlatan offered a magic potion--

One more elixir for eternal life?

One more raindrop fallen into the ocean.

It's no use questioning when or where--

As Rumi said, it's not your place to care;

You must be ready when the time is come,

The rest of life is only so much air.

There may be too many of these, as is,
And perhaps no need for another like this;
I know how this game of poetry goes--
Historically speaking, they're hit and miss.

I've spent my entire life on the fence about the value and relevance of poetry in the modern world—so, this is leaving a sponge in the patient, as it were. If I really thought these superfluous, why should I bother with them? And how would I know, either way?

Find happiness today, and every day--

For sorrows always come, and often stay;

Our tenure down here is transitory,

And once your story's told, you're on your way.

When we're again with family and friends,

And this accursed isolation ends,

We'll celebrate the simplest joys, although

No-one in charge will ever make amends.

I knew I was always pressing my luck,

Dodging my creditors, passing the buck--

And still, when it came time to pony up

For all that I've owed, I was thunderstruck.

This is intended in karmic terms, of course-
-however, it comes closer to home on a
literal level than I care to admit. Maybe, it's
true for most people, that we owe far more
to others than we realize (doesn't take me
off the hook, though...)

You walk on coals with typical abandon,

You're on the ledge with nothing soft to land on;

This life lends options, often slim to none,

And sometimes leaves you no safe place to stand on.

Under the big sky, there are still wild horses

Running the fields thunderous in their courses--

They rush relentless as a breaking wave,

As fierce as any elemental forces.

Nobody knows the object of this game,
Its limits or its eventual aim;
Winners aren't honored, and losers just gone,
And every round's conclusion ends the same.

Tomorrow will be better than today,
Redemption *must* be headed on its way--
It's such an easy, hopeful phrase to say,
When the only other option is to pray.

*This quatrain is harsher than I'd intended,
and I've questioned its inclusion. I think it's
valid, so I kept it—but I don't entirely share
its dark outlook.*

Astronomers citing how stars collapse,

How far existence stretches, til it snaps,

Still have a gap in all their starry charts--

They'll never locate Heaven on their maps.

I've stolen this from myself—that is, I wrote a sonnet several years ago about finding Heaven on a map; and, well, here it is again...curiously enough, the sonnet argues just the opposite.

Icicles line banisters thick with frost,

The snows obscure the lane—the way is lost;

Winter approaches in her icy coach,

As autumn's slow recession pays its cost.

The New Year pirouettes her hopeful dance,

And gives the old year not one backward glance;

The new year may be better, if we're lucky--

At least, it gives us all another chance.

I envy monks and nuns, who live so pure

Retreated from the outside world, so secure

In those beliefs that can never be proved--

I'd give up half my goods, to be so sure.

Now the day's ending, and the full moon throws

Patterns of silver over the folded rose--

Put out the candles where there's sleepers by,

For now the time's come for this book to close.

Now the day's ending, and the half moon throws

Patterns of silver on the folded rose--

Turn down the lanterns where there's sleepers by,

It's time now for this little book to close.